I Live in the Greatest Country

Dedicated to Liam and Susanna,
Who inspired me to write this book.

You are the future;
It's up to you to keep America
THE GREATEST COUNTRY.
Love, Pops

This book belongs to:

_____

an

AMERICAN PATRIOT

I Live in the Greatest Country!

by Fred Atkins

Fred Atkins

I live in the greatest country!
I live in the USA.

The United States of America,
I am very proud to say.

I live where I am free to do
whatever I want to do.

I can be whatever I want to be,
I can—and so can you.

The United States of America is the freest land there is.

No one can tell me what to say, or tell me where to live.

BALLOT BOX PRECINCT

I can go to church wherever I want
and I can go to school.

I can read any book I want to read,
no one can stop me, that's the rule.

It doesn't matter where I was born,
or matter what is my name.

It doesn't matter what color my skin,
everyone is treated the same.

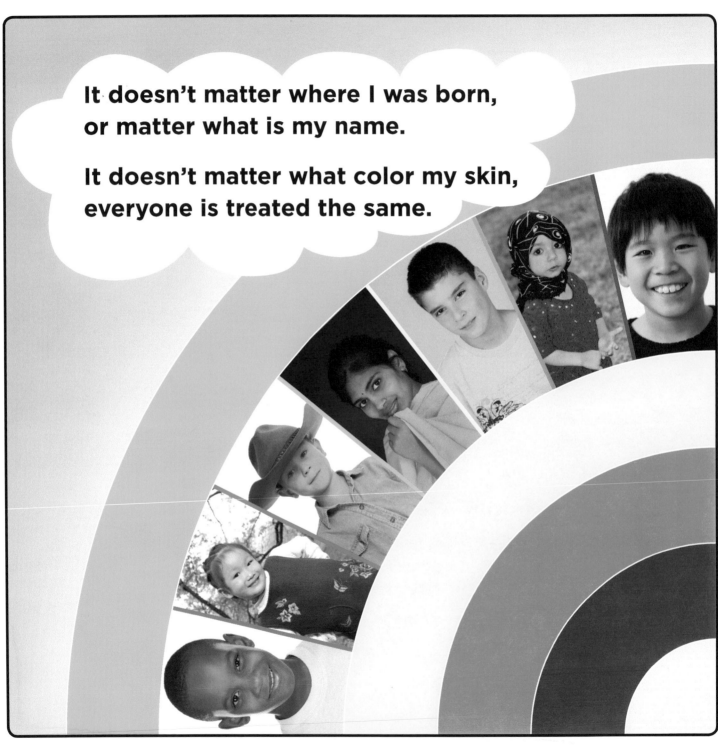

In the USA I can grow up to be anything I want to be,

But I know I'll have to work real hard—
it's up to ONLY ME.

It's not like that all over the world,
     in some places I wouldn't be free.

I'd have to hide just to read this book,
     if I were caught I'd have to flee.

There are places where you can't say what you think;
if you do, you get in trouble.

I wouldn't want to live there, would you?
I would leave—on the double!

There are people in other countries
who don't like the USA.

Sometimes they start a fight with us
to take our freedoms away.

December 7, 1941.
Japan attacks the United
States to start World War II

September 11, 2001.
Arab terrorists attack New York City

When they do, that's when we decide
that we will stand up and fight.

It's hard to do, but we do it,
because we know we are right.

The men and women who defend us
are the best in all our land.

Because of them we are safe tonight,
protected by their hand.

Many of them have fought and died to keep us safe and free.

We owe it to them to follow their lead and be the best that we can be.

We should not be afraid to fight for what's right
and to help those who cannot.

God made our country very strong
and he expects us to do a lot.

We should protect the weak and help the poor,
no matter where they may be.

That's the price Americans pay
for living in the Land of Liberty.

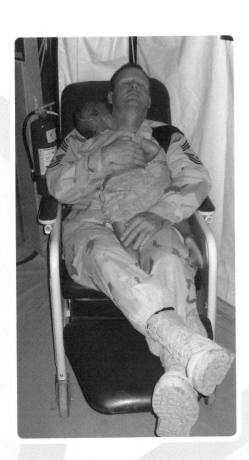

Yes, I live in the greatest country,

I live in the USA.

And I'm proud to say

I'm an American—

I'M AN AMERICAN,

I'M AN AMERICAN!

I'll shout it every day.

I LIVE IN THE GREATEST COUNTRY
is published by Children's Patriotic Press, Cary, North Carolina
www.patriotkidsUSA.com

Copyright © 2008 by Fred C Atkins Jr.
ISBN 978-0-9821172-0-0   Library of Congress PCN 2008909559

Photo credits:
Page 9 photo of Tiananmen Square courtesy of AP/WORLDWIDE PHOTOS
Page 10 photo of 9/11 attack on the twin towers courtesy of AP/WORLDWIDE PHOTOS
Page 10 photo of attack on Pearl Harbor courtesy of Department of Defense
Page 12 photos of military personnel courtesy of Department of Defense
Page 15 photo of aid to Bangladesh courtesy of USAID
Page 15 photo of John Gebhardt comforting Iraqi child courtesy of Department of Defense

IT'S NEVER TOO EARLY TO TEACH YOUR CHILD TO LOVE AMERICA

A Word from the author:

Don't just read this book to your children, <u>discuss</u> it with them. Talk about the words and the pictures and what they mean. Tell them your personal experiences and reflections. When you're out in the car with them, point out the flag, wave to policemen and firemen and talk about what they're doing to keep your family safe.

For more tips and suggestions on how to get the most out of this book, please go to our web site, www.PatriotKidsUSA.com and click on "getting the most."

Patriot Kids USA

Printed in the United States
140866LV00002B